GW00469448

LOSING MY
IDENTITY

MAGGIE MATTHEWS

BALBOA.PRESS

A DIVISION OF HAY HOUSE

Balboa Press books may be ordered through booksellers or by contacting:

Balboa Press
A Division of Hay House
1663 Liberty Drive
Bloomington, IN 47403
www.balboapress.co.uk
UK TFN: 0800 0148647 (Toll Free inside the UK)
UK Local: 02036 956325 (+44 20 3695 6325 from outside the UK)

Print information available on the last page.

ISBN: 978-1-9822-8355-1 (sc)
ISBN: 978-1-9822-8357-5 (hc)
ISBN: 978-1-9822-8356-8 (e)

Balboa Press rev. date: 06/10/2021

DEDICATION

*I dedicate this book to my children who I love
very much and am so proud of.*

CHAPTER 1

THE PERFECT FAMILY

On the outside, we were the perfect family.

Maggie and Lewis Matthews, and our two children, Luke and Lucy.

We managed our own successful roofing business, lived in a brand new house in the country and owned two properties abroad. We both drove new cars, and our children never wanted for anything.

At the time, Lewis was working on a number of different contracts and would employ people to work under him with each new project, as our business was expanded and grew with new clients.

What more could our family possibly want? Like I said, from the outside we had everything, and people used to say how lucky we were to live in such a beautiful home and be part of such a beautiful family.

It was the perfect life, lived by the perfect family. Lewis worked very hard putting long hours into the business; sometimes working 6 days a week, and always available at the end of a phone.

Meanwhile, I would manage the admin side of the business, booking in appointments and new contracts.

Sometimes Lewis would work away on new developments, sometimes he was home.

But he always made time for Lucy and Lewis, as family time was so important.

We played golf, went fishing and camping. We especially loved our holidays abroad, which we took at least twice a year, one in the winter, and one in the summer.

.

Eventually though, success and work began to take its toll on Lewis' health, he was exhausted and stressed. I suggested he took on more employees to work with him and support him, but he always claimed to enjoy the buzz of business and living on the edge, being in complete control.

He wouldn't trust anyone with the business he had worked so hard to set up, and trusted only himself to maintain his reputation.

What this meant was that time and time again, he would come home exhausted, with flu like symptoms saying his whole body ached.

He started to suffer from crippling headaches and feeling low.

He eventually went to the doctor's begrudgingly and was advised to take some time off.

The Doctor thought Lewis was burnt out on every level, both mentally and physically.

His body was telling him to slow down, but he wouldn't listen.

Lewis took just one weekend to rest and went back to work on the Monday like nothing had happened, despite still not feeling great.

It started to take its toll on him, and very soon that began to affect our family life.

Lewis became more irritable, angry, and short tempered.

He had no tolerance or patience with our children and would lose his temper at the slightest thing.

His mood swings were becoming more obvious and more frequent.

His body language told me he was constantly tired and tense.

His behaviour was not normal, and I suggested he went back to the doctors.

But Lewis said they were a waste of time.

Behind closed doors, our home, once so happy and full of life and love, became a very different place from the haven that everyone imagined.

It was sometimes a place of fear, of uncertainty, like we were constantly walking on eggshells.

But still Lewis held onto the image of the perfect family and perfect marriage and would pretend as if nothing was wrong whenever we saw or spoke to anyone else.

We were a young family with everything going for us and an amazing future.

Our children were involved in many activities and never went without.

Luke and Lucy had the latest games, clothes, mobile phones and sports equipment.

It seemed too good to be true, because it was.

Lewis's sleeping pattern started to change, he was restless, and he had trouble sleeping.

He would be awake most of the night and was constantly checking his phone, as if he couldn't switch off mentally.

He was working even longer hours and coming home later, blaming it on work and meetings.

His mood swings were becoming darker and more noticeable.

He was always angry and irritable.

Nothing seemed good enough anymore and he was criticising everything we did.

He was always making excuses to go out and meet people.

He stopped having family meals with us and said that he would eat later.

All the while his appetite was decreasing and his body language was growing increasingly tense.

Without even noticing, we became wary of him every single day, not knowing which Lewis would walk through the door when he finally arrived home.

I'll be honest with you, I thought he was having an affair!!

After all, what else could it be?

My gut feeling was telling me something was wrong, and his behaviour had made me suspicious.

Not only that, but I knew he was lying to me about where he had been and what he was doing.

I didn't know what to do or how to even begin to go about approaching the subject.

I had never had any issues of trust before, we had a good marriage.

What was happening?

What had gone wrong?

Then one night he came home late, and I thought to myself, there is something different about him.

He was suddenly very chilled. He was calm and overly affectionate; something I hadn't seen in a long time.

I asked him why he was so beaming like a Cheshire cat and where his energy had come from.

I said to him that over the last weeks and months he had been distant, unpredictable and angry. I asked outright, what's changed?

Then I blurted out the question that had been plaguing me: have you been having an affair?

Lewis just burst out laughing and said, when have I had the time?

But you have been coming home later and working longer hours.

I couldn't stop myself, I said, I don't believe you.

We started to argue, and he said simple that what I was saying was all in my head.

How do you explain your behaviour tonight, I hit back being so calm and relaxed?

Your voice is all croaky and your eyes are like pins.

You're scratching and sweaty.

Are you ill? Have you got a temperature?

He started to get angry at that and demanded me to stop asking so many questions.

Lewis was different and acting weird.

This went on for months, until even the children noticed the change in him.

Luke said to me one day out of the blue, there is something different about dad.

One minute he's nice and then he gets so angry, so quickly?

What's happening to him?

Why doesn't he spend as much time with us?

We hardly see him.

I could see the hurt in his eyes and could practically feel the rejection he felt, as he and his dad used to do so much together.

I felt angry, as I tried to keep my family together and hold onto a sense of normality.

Luke said there was always a funny smell around his dad, and that he kept breaking his promises to do stuff together.

I said I would have a chat with him and see if we could have a weekend away like we used too.

Lucy on the other hand wasn't affected as much, as she was younger.

But she did notice that he was different, as he used to read with her in the evenings but hadn't done this for months.

When she asked him to read with her, he was always too tired, or he didn't have enough time.

Again, he broke his promises to her anytime he said he would make it up to her.

I tried to make it up to them and compensate for their dad's behaviour.

I became more hands on, joining in with all of their activities, as Lewis wasn't around.

Our business, meanwhile, was successful and getting busier by the day.

I decided to ask around and try to speak to his work colleagues.

But men stick together, and nothing was disclosed.

I felt hurt, angry, confused and let down. Lewis was hiding something from me.

That or he was shutting me out and not letting me even try to understand what was going on.

He was starting to keep irregular hours, sleeping in later, staying out later.

But still he worked hard and finished his contracts.

I thought that if I became more relaxed over the situation, he might open up more, rather than me being on his case.

So that's what I did, but still, nothing changed or improved.

If anything, I noticed that the more freedom I gave him by not asking questions, the more relaxed he became.

I think he thought that I accepted what was going on, which suited him.

With the freedom came a level of arrogance I didn't like, as I felt we were living separate lives.

Lewis thought I would accept and stay with him because of what we had financially, our business and our children.

He knew I would do anything to keep the family together, but this was pushing the boundaries.

I was nobody's fool.

As time went on, his behaviour worsened.

His pupils were like pins anytime his eyes looked into mine.

He was sweating and scratching all the time.

He had a horrible metal smell on his clothes.

He was full of energy, acting happy, very affectionate and attentive to me and the children, which was out of character.

I didn't know what was happening, just like I didn't understand this change in him and his personality.

I asked him what was going on, why was he out all the time and why his personality continued to change. He said simple that nothing had changed, and nothing was going on, and that I must be imagining it all.

I felt as if as I going mad, especially with all the lies that followed.

Lewis was lying about everything, but I could pinpoint nothing.

And then I started to notice money going missing from our business bank account.

I asked him for receipts to prove what he was spending it on, to put through the business.

I needed them to support our expenditure for tax purposes.

He just got angry, would lose his temper. and said that he could spend it on what he wanted, as he worked hard for it.

He expressed his belief that I had enough money to live on and to pay the bills, what more could I want!!

Two to three hundred pounds a week was being spent, but on what?

There was nothing to show for it.

He would disappear all night and come home at all different hours of the night.

I also noticed that my kitchen foil kept disappearing. I put it down to the children making things.

But this became a weekly thing.

His sweating got worse, and that terrible metallic smell seemed to be everywhere he went.

In his car, in his van, even in our garage.

Then one day he was getting out of the shower and I noticed he had pinpricks on certain parts of his body near his veins.

I have never seen anything like it before, what the hell was it?

I asked him what they were, but he became angry and defensive and said he had always had them.

I became so distraught and worried, I had to talk to someone and find out what was going on.

I was naive and felt my whole world had turned upside down.

I spoke to a friend who I knew was streetwise and told her what was going on.

I explained about his changed behaviour, the constant sweating with its horrible odour, the foil and money going missing. Staying out all night and those pinpricks on certain parts of his body.

My friend knew straight away, and explained that Lewis was on drugs, most probably injecting himself, which would explain the pinprick marks.

I was horrified. I could not believe what I was hearing. I was devastated, angry, shocked, and felt like I had been kicked in the stomach.

I didn't know anything about drugs.

I felt like an idiot and like I was being taken for one by my own husband.

But WHY?

What was the need for drugs, he had everything? Or at least I thought so.

I couldn't understand any of this, I was so upset, and I felt my whole life had just turned upside down.

What was I going to do? What about the children?

My husband was a drug addict, my children's dad was a drug addict!!

I couldn't believe what I was telling myself.

Was this for real?

I was suddenly living a nightmare which I wanted to wake up from but couldn't.

I decided to wait up and confront Lewis that night and find out the truth.

To finally find out what was really going on.

I was feeling sick and trembling but knew I had to stay calm and not let the children sense or see that anything was wrong.

The children had their evening meal and went to relax.

Meanwhile, I tidied up and sat with a glass of wine and waited for Lewis.

As Lewis came through the door that evening, he was surprised to see me.

I thought you would be in bed. No I decided to wait up as I need to talk to you.

Lewis said innocently, can't it wait until tomorrow?

No, I said calmly. I need to know if you're taking drugs and injecting.

His face dropped and his body language became tense.

Where did you get that idea from?

I listed the reasons. From your behaviour, smell, the money going missing and the pin pricks marks on your body.

I said you have changed so much, you're not the man I married.

Your distant and secretive, you have no interest in family life, you only do what you want.

The children have noticed a change in you and feel nervous around you.

Lewis became furious, saying how hard he worked for all of us and that even if he was doing drugs, what did it matter?

He still paid the bills and continued with the contracts and business.

I stayed calm. So, you're admitting that you are?

Only every now and again, he stated. It helps me chill and it helps when my body aches…like a pain relief.

I couldn't believe it, I was in shock, as I was expecting he would deny it as always.

I said, trembling, what drug are you taking?

Lewis said why do you need to know, it shouldn't affect us!

I laughed. What, are you mad?

Have you not heard anything I have said about how we feel, and how your children have noticed that you've changed?

You have ignored the family and put yourself and your drugs first.

We have been put in last place and forgotten.

We argued, but nothing was resolved as Lewis truly thought he was doing nothing wrong.

Lewis finally admitted that he was taking Heroin and that the drugs were what the money was being spent on from the business account.

I knew nothing about Heroin, but I knew it was addictive and I knew enough to understand that it ruined people's lives.

I didn't want any part of it and I gave him an ultimatum, that if he gave it up, I would support him and help him.

But I couldn't be married to a heroin addict. I had already had a taste of what life would be like and knew it would only get worse.

The mood swings, living on the edge, never knowing when or if he was coming home.

The amount of money that was disappearing from the business account.

It was having a major effect on all of us on a mental, emotional, and physical level.

This drug habit had been going on for months, and I had stupidly thought he was having an affair.

I think, now, that an affair might have been easier to accept. How do you compete with heroin?

Heroin had taken its toll with Lewis and he had become dependant on it.

I had to make a decision based on what was best for me and my children. Lewis wouldn't accept that this was a problem, and believed that as long as he worked, and the business thrived, he could afford his habit.

I hated what he was doing to our family, but he couldn't see it.

He was angry, shouting and swearing and saying that I would be the one to split the family up. That it would be my fault.

After all, wasn't I was the one being demanding and asking him to give it up or get out?

CHAPTER 2

THE BEGINNING OF THE END

The children's father came, as usual, to pick them up one day a week… that's if it suited him.

My son would go with him, but my daughter would not, as she wanted to stay with me and as she did not feel safe with him.

That was my fault, of course. It always was.

Luke was 13 years old, and Lucy was just 10. Too young to see what she had seen years old.

As our family unit had dissipated, it became more and more obvious that Lewis would not accept the separation.

Lewis could not accept that, even though he had kept the business going and had carried on bringing money into our family, being the main provider that I would not accept at his way of life surrounded by involving drugs.

Lewis had changed beyond belief, he wasn't the man I had married and certainly was not the man that I had loved.

Lewis tried to promised me that he would only do the drugs outside the house, so Luke and Lucy would not know.

But how could they not know, with his personality changing bothe when he was high or coming down!

His mood swings and his disappearances affected us all and he couldn't even see it for days and coming in late.

Lewis would argue that said I had everything and wanted for nothing, and that so he couldn't see what the problem was.

The fact that what he was doing was illegal, telling me constant lies, and removing the trust that had been built upon, meant nothing to him.

I became a nervous wreck, living on the edge, not knowing what would happen next or how his mood swings would affect me and the children.

I spent my days trying to keep the peace and have minimum disruption within the household.

All the while I was protecting the children as much as I could from their dad and his drug habit.

Luke and Lucy couldn't understand his extreme behavior and felt scared increasingly regularly sometimes.

Lewis was spending less time at home and less time with his family.

As we drifted further apart, I went to see a solicitor to start proceedings, as I knew I had to move towards a divorce.

I didn't like Lewis or his behaviour. I didn't know him anymore.

But in my heart I still loved the old Lewis and desperately wanted him back.

The drugs had taken over him from me, and now controlled all his decisions.

Once Lewis knew I had been to the solicistors though, the whole scenario became worse.

He said he would make my life hell, just as I had done by filing for a divorce.

Lewis told me he would not leave the family home until he was ready, and that he wanted a settlement from the house. He told me, in no uncertain terms, that I would receive nothing from the business.

He said that I wouldn't receive any help from him in any way, shape, or form.

If I wanted a divorce, I could have one but I would be left to support myself.

Lewis would not accept responsibility for his actions or choices.

Drugs had done this to Lewis, ruining our life from a distance.

Lewis even tried to accused me of having an affair, stating that that was the reason why I wanted a divorce.

That was a lie, but Lewis did anything he could to blame someone or something.

His behavior was spiralling out of control.

My son, Luke, missed his father terribly after the divorce when Lewis eventually left the family home.

Lewis was always asking him what I was doing and if I was seeing anyone else. Luke used to say to me, whenever he saw his dad, that after being with his dad that Lewis just wanted to come home.

Luke would tell me that his dad was sorry for all the things he had done. Luke said that his dad told him he was a sick man and that I should have him back.

My son enjoyed his time with his dad but when he came home he was always very angry and upset, as his dad wanted him to persuade me to let him move back home.

This manipulation made my son very angry with me, and I constantly got the blame for breaking up the family home.

I got the blame for his dad's illness.

I asked him to remember what had happened and why we had to separate.

I told my son that his dad is not ill, he was on drugs!!

He was a Heroin addict. It was the Heroin talking, not his dad.

When he was on drugs, he was nice, but when he was coming down or withdrawing, he was angry, violent, and unpredictable. We all lived in fear of his actions.

His mood swings would change as quickly as switching on a switch.

I would be walking on eggshells every minute of every day, and could not reason with him.

If he couldn't have his own way, or if I did not agree with what he said, he would become vindictive and violent.

He would throw things, sometimes trashing an entire room in the house. He would use words that were hurtful, and which was designed to destroy my confidence.

He would break Luke's games if he didn't behave and had even ended up hitting him once or twice, with whatever he had in his hands at the time.

If I tried to stop him or intervene, he said that Luke would get it twice as hard and that I would be next.

I had been pinned up against the wall with his hands around my throat while begging him to stop hitting Luke, just for answering back.

But Luke was a teenager, didn't they misbehave from time to time?

This man was supposed to be their father, protecting them, having fun and playing with them.

Showing them love and keeping them safe.

But Lewis was our very own Jekyll and Hyde.

He was like a time bomb waiting to go off.

On the drugs, he was calm, loving and always happy. But when he was withdrawing or coming down, that was when his character began to change.

This wasn't just occasional, or even regular. It was happening 7 days a week, 24 hours a day, for 12 months. 365 days of not knowing what each day was going to bring.

I could not take it anymore. It was affecting my children, and I wanted them to feel safe and loved.

I had to file for divorce citing unreasonable behavior!!

But I also feared for my life.

My husband could not understand why I could and would not accept his drug-taking.

I did not want Luke and Lucy to be raised by a heroin addict, I wanted, him to be a proper father and to be a normal family like we used to be... or to not be there at all.

Was that too much to ask?

CHAPTER 3

THE SEPARATION

The time I found myself filing for a divorce and waiting for everything to be finalized, became the longest and hardest wait of my life.

Time seemed to stand still, the solicitors were taking their time to do the paperwork, and everything was moving slower than I had ever imagined. Or so it felt, anyway.

Our lives became worse as Lewis simply would not accept the separation or divorce proceedings. Lewis vowed that he would make my life hell, just as he claimed I had done with my wanting a divorce, and so he refused to leave the family home.

He said why he should leave, as he wasn't doing anything wrong.

Lewis wasn't going anywhere without the settlement he wanted.

He told me, in no uncertain terms, that would decide when he was leaving and there was nothing I could do about it.

Until that time, he kept true to his word, and life became unbearable. His mood swings affected all of us and I told the children to try their best to and behave around their dad. We didn't know how he was going to react, whether he would be argumentative or he would become aggressive and destructive with furniture.

Even Luke's PlayStation became the subject of violence, when Lewis picked it up and threw it across the room because his son dared to answered him back.

But Luke was just a teenager, he was struggling and angry himself, scared of what his dad had become. Lewis made sure that both Lucy and Luke knew that I was the one wanting the divorce and splitting the family up.

Unbeknown to me Lewis was, by now, travelling to big cities to buy his heroin and was selling it from our property.

Still naive and vulnerable I was told that these buyers were business associates coming to talk business and view the goods!!

I confronted him once and said couldn't he do business during the day and hold meetings at unreasonable times during the day.

Lewis replied this was another type of business he was doing and just smirked.

He said he could make a week's money in a day, and that his new business was far better than working hard all week.

I didn't understand what he meant, and didn't want to know. As I knew it would be dodgy.

I was always cleaning to get rid of the awful smell, as he would burn it and inhale his drugs in the downstairs toilet.

One time I found a plastic tub with the drugs in, down behind the toilet cistern with needles. I asked him to at least keep it outside the house because the children could have found it and he must know how dangerous it would have been for them.

I was going out of my mind with worry and didn't know how to handle this in the best way for all of us.

I was living in fear, all the while trying and tried to keep the peace and be calm and strong.

Lewis only laughed in my face saying it would have been my fault if the children were harmed, for not doing what he wanted.

He would come and go as he pleased and the atmosphere was intense and depressing.

Lewis treated the home as a hotel and left a mess where ever he went.

He would disappear for days on end and suddenly reappear on a high, or withdrawing that was when the dark angry side would appear.

His hygiene was declining as was his self-respect, his clothes were always dirty and he looked as if he was losing weight rapidly.

The house started to smell of heroin again, and it made me feel dirty. The life I was living went totally against my morals, judgement, and beliefs.

I kept quiet through fear though, hoping that if I let him lead his own life, he would find someone else and leave the children and me alone.

But he did both, he enjoyed bragging about the other woman he was sleeping with and revelling in the fact he could have the best of both worlds, as I was his still wife and had to uphold my duties. Lewis said it wasn't his problem, because this was my doing.

His main concern was having what he wanted and living his life the way he wanted too, destroying whoever or whatever got in his way.

He still kept trying to persuade me to change my mind and told me that if I did what he said I could have what I want, and life could return to normal!

Not only that, but he said we would have more money than before as he was dealing and as well as running our business.

Now I understood what he meant when he had said that he could earn more money in a day than he could working hard all week.

He was also a Dealer!!

How could things get any worse?

I wanted to cry, I was exhausted, and truly felt I was at my lowest.

But how could I refuse with all the money he was making, that's what women wanted, didn't they?? That was what he said to me. He said there was something wrong with me, that I was mentally ill or I was having an affair? That's what he wanted, as it would be so much easier for him to have someone to blame for his behaviour.

All I wanted was to have a peaceful, quiet family life where we all felt loved and safe.

Lewis said that I could not cope and could not live without him, as I was pathetic, weak, fat and ugly and no-one else would want me.

He said I would not be able to afford the mortgage and pay all the bills, without him, that I needed him.

He said you cannot survive without me, you will be begging me to come back.

That I was the selfish one, I must be seeing someone else as I was the one filing for divorce.

That it was my fault that he was taking drugs and for his behaviour.

That I should have been more supportive and understanding.

Whatever he demanded he got, with or without my consent, as we were still husband and wife.

I was so desperate for him to leave, I was crying both inside and out.

I felt like a robot, I was on autopilot and started to feel dead inside.

I was walking on eggshells and living in fear, trying to protect my children from what was going on inside our house once a happy family home.

I had to try and stay strong and remember that this was only temporary, and that when the money came and he had his settlement, he would be finally out of my life.

My solicitor advised me to re mortgage the house, to give Lewis the agreed financial settlement.

I wanted this to be over as quickly as possible, but my solicitor advised me that Lewis would not go quietly due to his character.

My bank were very supportive, and I found a way of re mortgaging with an interest-only mortgage which I could change back to repayment once I got back on my feet.

I felt relieved that I had found a way to do this, and Lewis was very surprised when I told him that he would have his money soon. Lewis also agreed that he would sign over the house to me and sign the divorce papers once he received his settlement. But he was angry and shocked that I managed to get the house signed over and re mortgaged. He thought I would never be able to do it and assumed that I would have to sell the house eventually and downsize as I wouldn't be able to afford the mortgage. In my head I knew I would work all the hours I needed to keep this house and the children safe. I had found a part time job but I hadn't told Lewis as he still wanted me to do the admin and books for the business, which I would do on the side as it meant I could take a wage from the business.

But eventually I knew I wanted to be totally independent and free from Lewis and the business, as while I worked there it still gave him a form of control over me. It meant I would still be part of his life and him in mine which I didn't want. I didn't trust him like I used too, in business or as a wife. I think he thought I would always be beholding to him, which is what he wanted.

I was desperate now. I knew the end was near, and I couldn't wait for him to leave the family home.

But the end couldn't come soon enough, as one particular night his arrogance, coldness and anger came out in a way that would haunt me for a long time.

I never knew how much strength I needed until this one particular night, which came to be one of the worst I had experienced in my life.

I heard the door open in the early hours of the morning and heard his footsteps coming up the stairs, I froze and pretended I was asleep.

Lewis got into bed next to me and pushed me, all I could smell was whisky and I could tell he was high, surrounded with that metallic smell and whispering in a croaky voice.

He rolled me over and climbed on top of me, saying he had marital rights and was going to cash them in here and now.

I tried to push him off, struggling with his weight and the heaviness of his body, but he just pinned me down, I felt as if I was suffocating, as I wanted to scream, but no noise came. I just froze and thought of the children.

I kept quiet and let him do what he wanted as I thought it would be over quickly…, but I was wrong.

I didn't want to wake the children up and for them to see this, and what their dad was capable of.

His body was hot and sweaty as he forced his hardness inside of me and pushed aggressively, over and over again, hurting me while he took, what he called his marital rights, again and again until the sun came up.

It felt like, it went on for hours because it did, his heavy body pumping at mine while I was crying, feeling disgusted, weak and pathetic.

Perhaps he was right, that I was weak and pathetic.

I hated myself even more now, for letting him do this to me.

I felt sick, bruised, swollen, sore, and humiliated.

The sun was rising when he finally rolled over to the other side of the bed and fell asleep.

I got into the shower, my whole body was aching, bruised and tender. I was crying quietly.

I scrubbed myself so hard trying to get his smell off my body. I felt dirty and cheap.

I got dressed and had to put a brave, smiley face on for my children, trying my best to erase what happened a few hours ago from my mind and my memory.

I couldn't stop shaking and I felt exhausted, my mind was shattered but I had to stay strong and get through this.

I couldn't tell anyone as I was terrified. I felt numb, but who would believe me?

We were the perfect family, and he was the most charismatic and charming person you could meet. I had once believed myself to be so lucky.

Now, I couldn't believe that someone who was supposed to love you and want to be with you, could do that to you.

The love I had once held for him had started to turn to hate.

Fear and control replaced the love he promised me.

Yet he continued to force me to believe that this was my fault, that I deserved this, and if I did as I was told, it would not have happened.

I was leading a double life, one for the outside world to see and a completely different one behind closed doors.

How much longer could I keep this up? I did not know.

I had become a nervous wreck and was losing weight, finding it hard to eat or sleep.

I had to keep it together for the children and keep quiet.

Nobody would believe me anyway.

This went on for 5 months, until finally, the settlement arrived.

I managed to re mortgage the house on an interest only mortgage so we could stay in the family home.

Money was transferred and the divorce papers were signed.

My now ex-husband Lewis was laughing and was happy to leave. He had what he wanted and looked to all the world like the cat who had got the cream and more.

As he signed the divorce papers, he was gloating, saying that I would need him long before he needed me.

No one would ever want me or look at me again. I would not be able to survive without him. Lewis continued to tell me that he would not support the children or give me any maintenance for them, as I chose this life, so I could have it.

He wanted me to fail and see me in the gutter.

He would see the children on his terms as and when he wanted.

And that's what he did, not caring about their feelings, when he was let down.

The false promises and hopes that he made to him, followed by the excuses for not turning up whenever plans had been organised.

Lewis was simply too busy with his new life of sex, drugs and being a dealer, making money.

I managed to get more hours and went from part –time to full –time employment, working in an office and doing various admin tasks, which I was what I was used to. I left the business solely to Lewis.

He could employ someone else to do the books, as I wanted no part of his life and nothing to do with him.

I knew it would only be a matter of time before our once thriving business went downhill. The signs were already there.

His reputation was no longer as good as it used to be, and he was not turning up on site anymore. Not only that but the contractors were starting to hear rumours about his habit.

Pretty soon, he wasn't getting any new contracts anymore, and new business started to dry right up.

But that wasn't my concern anymore, I had to concentrate on me and the children.

Returning to a normal family life of peace and quiet became my sole goal.

Feeling safe in my own home, and allowing Luke and Lucy to be able to be themselves again and have their friends over once again, became my lifeline.

CHAPTER 4

ONE YEAR LATER

As time went on, Lewis lost the business and became a full-time dealer.

He was spending over £350.00 a week on his habit every week and was earning more money than he ever had before through his legitimate business.

By this time, Lewis had also been in numerous relationships, all with much younger women.

But still he resented the fact that I was working full-time, and was managing to pay the mortgage by myself.

I had found a way to balance my work life and home life, discovering that even though it was hard work, it was worth it.

I would drop Lucy off at Breakfast Club and Luke would walk to school with his friends.

I would then collect Lucy from Afterschool Club and would get home at 6 pm.

From there, my evenings were spent cooking dinner and helping them both with their homework.

Life was quiet, peaceful and we were living a normal family life, as far as we could.

I was free, independent and happy.

Lucy was happy and content.

Luke was getting along, but still he was angry and missed having his dad around. The few times he spoke to me about how he felt, I discovered, he felt confused and wanted us to be like his friends' families.

But still, I felt proud that I was managing to get by without any help from Lewis and was starting to feel safe and calm in my family home.

I could finally have a peaceful night's sleep, without being woken up in fear.

I could lock my front door and feel safe.

We all started to relax and enjoy life.

Life became better overwith time, and we all established a good routine that worked.

Luke still saw his dad, but it was always as and when it suited Lewis.

Lewis would ring up at last minute and make an excuse not to see him.

Usually, these excuses revolved around working late, but I knew it was because of either drugs or women.

During these calls, Lewis would speak to Luke and would promise to make it up to him and see him through the week instead.

I constantly told Lewis how upset and disappointed Luke was, but he brushed it off and said he would be fine.

Luke wasn't fine, he was gutted and angry.

And I would get the brunt of the blame from both of them.

Lewis used to say I chose this living situation, so I had to deal with it.

Luke, meanwhile, said that dad was ill, and I should take him back, proclaiming that, it was my fault!!

Lewis used to constantly ask Luke what I was doing and who I was seeing. Who came to the house?

Luke would say Mum just works all the time and her girlfriends come to the house sometimes.

Lewis kept asking if there was another man on the scene, but there wasn't.

He found it hard to accept that I was happier on my own than with him, and would not believe Luke.

He still wanted to believe there was someone else so he could have someone to blame.

Lewis was living in a state of denial, unable to understand that it was his choice to do the drugs and that the lifestyle he chose came at a price.

That lifestyle had split us up.

He could not understand that I was happy being single, and that every day I came home being shattered from working full-time and running around after the children and all their activities.

He kept saying I should be looking after him.

But I already had 2 children, I didn't want a third.

The visits and telephone calls became less frequent.

Luke used to ring his dad but even he, over time, he became fed up with the lies and empty promises.

Luke was a teenager and wanted to be one, spending time with all his friends.

My children were settled and getting stronger.

At the back of my mind, I did think it was strange how Lewis had disappeared, as Lewis was never quiet, there was always drama wherever he went.

I just thought, for once, that maybe no news really is good news.

Maybe he had actually moved on and settled down in a relationship.

One night, after about a week of no contact, Lewis started to send me some dark, destructive self-obsessive, abusive, vindictive, and threatening texts.

I ignored them, hoping and assuming that it was the drugs and drink talking.

But they carried on, into the early hours of the morning.

Then the phone calls started, saying how much pain he was in and how much he was suffering.

He did not want to live anymore and I had to suffer and die with him!

He could not endure the pain anymore and was going to make me suffer, just as he had.

I was going to feel what it was like to be in so much pain…

I was terrified, my heart was pounding and I was trying to reason with him…

Trying to make him see sense, explaining that our children needed their dad.

But Lewis kept saying they would be better off without him.

That they didn't care as they hadn't called him all week.

I explained that they were children and they were busy with their friends.

But in my head, I knew they hadn't called because they were angry. He kept letting them down, it was his fault, not theirs. But I couldn't say it.

I didn't want to make him any angrier than he was.

I could tell he had been drinking and was high on heroin.

His voice was croaky and slurred.

I said calmly that he was depressed, and I would help him to get through it.

He said that unless I took him back, he was going to come to the house.

I said it was the middle of the night and the children were asleep.

I'm coming to the house, so get the children up!

I felt sick and was shaking, hoping that he couldn't drive.

I decided to try and get some sleep, but my mind was racing and the fear was rising.

He had had suicidal thoughts before, and I was hoping that this was all it was.

An hour or so passed and suddenly there is a loud knocking on the front door.

I was trembling as I went downstairs slowly, the loud knocking on the door was continuous and unrelenting.

This is not good, my gut instinct was terrified and on red alert, my whole body was shaking.

I just knew something really bad was going to happen, so I started to pray.

If there is a God, please keep us all safe.

I opened the door and he pushed his way in...

Lewis was high as a kite and stank of alcohol.

His eyes were diluted and his pupils like pins, his clothes were filthy and his whole body language was filled with rage.

Where were the kids?

In bed of course, but they were awake now and wondering what was going on.?

Lewis told us all to get upstairs and told the kids that they wouldn't see me again.

He told them we were going to die, that he was going to kill me then himself...

He said to say goodbye to mum, as you will never see her again.

Luke and Lucy started crying and screaming; and asking why and was begging him not to...

Lewis said that he couldn't bear another man touching me or the children having another dad.

He said that if he couldn't have me, nobody else could. That, I would have to die if I didn't take him back.

I was crying and begging him to realise what he was saying and surely, he didn't mean it.

Lewis told the children to go to bed and told Luke to look after his sister.

The next thing I knew, I saw his fist coming towards my face.

I fell to the floor and all I can remember is being punched and kicked, over and over. I think I must have passed out as I went into darkness.

Then I felt my hair being pulled, my body being dragged and thrown across the floor, hitting the radiator.

Being picked up again and being thrown against the cupboards, all the while while being punched and kicked senseless.

Everything happened so quickly and I was going in and out of consciousness.

All of a sudden it stopped, and I didn't know where I was, if I was dead or alive.

I lay on the floor in darkness.

I heard the door open and Luke and Lucy came running in.

I heard Luke and Lucy's voices screaming Mum, Mum.

I tried to open my eyes, but only one eye would open, the other hads closed over.

I felt numb, my whole body was aching and throbbing. I was afraid to move.

I could taste and feel blood everywhere on my body

Luke and Lucy helped me onto the bed, my head was banging and the pain was shooting all over my body like electric shocks.

Lewis was punching the door with his fists. He was hitting the door so hard that his fist went right through the door.

Luke asked what he was doing. Lewis said it was better than punching my face!

In my head, I was begging God to let me stay alive so I could keep my children safe.

Please, if there is a God or an Angel, please protect us and let this be just a nightmare that we would wake up from.

I will do anything to stay alive, Luke and Lucy need me.

Luke and Lucy helped me lie down on the bed and put a throw over me.

I couldn't stop shaking and trembling. I couldn't speak.

Lewis told them to go back to bed and leave us.

They asked their dad to promise not to hurt me anymore. No, they didn't ask. They begged.

Luke age 13, and Lucy age 10. What they had just witnessed must have felt like being in a horror movie. I couldn't imagine what they were going through.

They were children, I am supposed to keep them safe and protect them.

All I could hear was them crying and screaming for me.

I sensed Lewis laying down on the bed next to me, repeating that no-one was going to have me except him.

I felt his hands on my thighs, and pushing my nightdress up over my body.

He pushed me onto my side and opened my legs.

I lay still, rigid, frozen in fear, crying inside but unable to speak and too weak to fight him off.

I had to stay alive, so I lay still like a slab of marble.

Lewis started to rape me…

Luke came in as it went quiet, to check that I was still alive.

He was screaming Mum; Dad what are you doing to Mum?

Luke saw his dad raping me!

Lewis told him to get out and close the door.

Luke asked his dad why he was having sex with me. After what you have done to her?

Lewis got up from the bed and told Luke to go and get some cleaning cloths and cold water.

Get Lucy and she can help you clean up the mess in the bedroom.

To clean the blood from the radiators, the cupboards and the carpet.

I couldn't move, I couldn't speak. I think I was in shock.

I lay on the bed as if I was dead.

Luke and Lucy kept saying Mum, Mum wake up…

I knew I had to stay alive, I tried my hardest to move, I wanted them to know I was still here.

They were crying hysterically, and I could hear them shouting about how much blood there was everywhere.

I heard Lewis telling them to go to bed and telling them that I would be ok in the morning.

Luke and Lucy kissed my head and said love you, Mum.

I just moved my head slightly to acknowledge what they had said.

I was drifting in and out of consciousness.

Then, I passed out.

CHAPTER 5

BEING HELD, HOSTAGE

I woke up and the house was silent. As I tried to lift my head off the pillow, the pain was excruciating.

My whole body was bruised and throbbing, and every time I moved, the pain was everywhere.

Quietly the door opened, and Luke and Lucy came into the bedroom, asking and asked if I was ok?

I nodded, though I could only see out of one eye, as the other eye was totally swollen up and over.

Lucy started to cry, as she looked down onto my face which was bruised and swollen.

My head was banging, but I had to get up. My whole body felt like a dead weight.

I asked where their Dad was.

Luke said he was downstairs.

I said we have to get dressed and get you both to school.

I didn't know what day or time it was, but I had to get us out of the house.

Luke said that Dad said we are not going to school and that we all have to stay at home.

He said that his Father demanded I ring the school and say that both children are sick.

Looking at his feet, Luke said we are not allowed to go out and we're not allowed to tell anyone what happened.

At that moment, Lewis came upstairs with a cup of tea and some paracetamol.

I felt sick as fear rose up inside me when I saw him.

I said my head was hurting and I should see a doctor.

Lewis said you're not going anywhere, you will be fine.

I will take care of you.

He said to ring the school and say that we were all sick.

None of you is going anywhere, the doors are locked, and you're locked in.

Luke, Lucy and I cuddled up on the bed crying and sobbing.

Lewis announced that he was going to the shop to get some more painkillers and some food.

I am taking the keys with me, so you will be locked in.

I felt dead inside, needing to get in the shower and scrub myself, I wanted to get clean.

As I got off the bed, I looked around the bedroom and was shocked to see how much blood there was.

The bedsheets were covered in blood, plus the cupboards, and radiator and some on the carpet.

I thought I was going to faint, and felt myself go lightheaded.

As I got into the shower, the hot water cleansed my aching and bruised body.

The water hurt my body as it bounced on my skin, washing the dried blood away.

I gently dried myself slowly and gently while Lucy helped me to get dressed, as it was too painful to stretch.

I asked them both to strip the bed and to throw the bedding away. I didn't want anything in the house as a reminder of what happened.

Lucy helped to remake the bed, while Luke cleaned the cupboards and radiator of blood.

I had to stay strong and focused, I had to survive.

Lewis returned from the shop with treats for Luke and Lucy.

Flowers, wine, magazines, and chocolates for me.

Lewis started apologising and saying how sorry he was, would I forgive him?!

He was begging me for forgiveness and could not believe what he had done to me.

I was in a state of shock and could not believe what he was saying.

I nodded my head, as I was in fear and just wanted to stay alive.

I wanted to get through this terrible nightmare. At that point, I knew I would agree to say and do anything if it meant staying alive and to being with my children.

Lewis laid out his terms. Luke and Lucy had to behave and stay at home.

They couldn't go out to play and couldn't speak to their friends.

We were hostages in our home.

Lewis stayed with us, the days passing in a blur.

By this point, I wasn't sure what day it was. Lewis had taken to smoking the heroin inside the house.

I could smell that metallic smell everywhere, and would beg him not to do it in front of the children.

You could smell the heroin burning, hear the foil being ripped and the smell would fill the house.

It disgusted me and made me feel dirty. Just like before.

He would go into the downstairs toilet and come out sweating, scratching, his eyes like pins.

His personality changed so much, from being angry, irritable, and aggressive to placid, loving and attentive.

Lewis didn't care that we were inhaling the fumes, or that his children knew that he was a heroin addict.

I saw that Jekyll and Hyde personality return, created by the drugs which dominated us all while we tried trying to play happy families.

Luke was always on his PlayStation while Lucy hid in her bedroom, watching tv and colouring.

All I did was rest, I felt like I was afraid to move or have a voice. I kept quiet and prayed that I would heal as quickly as possible.

I lived on paracetamol and ibuprofen, I couldn't eat and felt constantly sick.

I couldn't stop trembling and had trouble sleeping.

The pain was slowly easing and my face and body has taken on the colours of a rainbow.

The bruising had come out fully with the swelling.

I felt so fragile and so alone, thinking that this was what goes on in films, not in real life.

Not in my reality anyway.

My work rang me and asked if everything was ok as they hadn't heard from me in a couple of days.

I said that I was ill and was not sure when I would be back.

My supervisor sensed there was something more, she sensed something was wrong, but I couldn't talk as Lewis was in the house.

Lewis kept saying that we must not tell anyone what happened, or he would finish off what he did the other night.

When my friends called, I had to act and pretend that I had been ill and I was on the mend.

They all knew that something wasn't right, but I stressed that everything was fine.

They wanted to come round and support me, but I told them to stay away and not to trouble themselves.

I didn't want anyone to know what he did or what happened.

I felt ashamed, guilty, and pathetic that the children had been put through this ordeal and that I could not stand up to him. That I had let him do this to me.

I felt disgusted with myself that I let him have sex with me.

I felt repelled at what Luke had seen.

I felt powerless that I had lost control and all sense of normality.

I wanted to get back to normal, whatever normality is…

I didn't know how or when this nightmare was going to end.

By this time a week had passed and I was becoming more mobile.

The pain was subsiding, and my swelling was starting to ease.

I could finally see out of my other eye and my body didn't ache as more.

Then, out of the blue, Lewis said he was going home and that the children could go back to school tomorrow, on the condition that they didn't say anything.

We all promised, at this point, we would have agreed to anything.

Relief washed over us, as he said he would phone us every day to check on us.

The main reason he was going home was that he needed to get his fix.

He had to go and score and buy his drugs, as he had used up his stash.

As Lewis walked out of the house, he closed the door behind him and got in his van.

I watched him drive away and as we watched his van go out of sight, I sat down and I cried uncontrollably.

Luke and Lucy hugged me and I told them how sorry I was.

We all cried with relief, sadness, and anger.

Luke told me it wasn't my fault; that it's the drugs!

We were all exhausted from living in fear and living on the edge, not knowing what to expect next.

Not knowing if Lewis would explode, releasing his dark side, or if he would be Mr Nice Guy for a while.

Lewis' life now was drugs and he was ruled by them.

He had now stepped over the mark, he made his bed and now he must lie in it.

He had lost control and there was no going back.

So sad, how love turns to hate so easily just because of someone's behaviour.

Lewis had it all and now it was gone.

Lewis had lost everything.

CHAPTER 6

BEING ESCORTED THROUGH THE NIGHT

Monday morning came, and I knew that in my diary there was a full team meeting for the company I was employed by.

I didn't have to go but I wanted to, as I wanted to get back to normal as quickly as possible.

I wanted our routine to resume quickly and, most of all, to forget what had happened.

But as I looked in the mirror, I knew I couldn't forget how could I?

My face was still a mass of bruising, covered in black, yellow and purple marks, and still swollen in a few places.

I started to put my make up on slowly and gently as my face was still tender, trying to cover up the bruises.

But no matter how much I put on, the bruises shone through.

I did the best I could, and when I was finished I thought I looked reasonable.

I started to get dressed in my usual black trouser suit and roll neck jumper, but to my shock, the trousers hung from me. I couldn't believe the weight I had lost in justwithin 7 days.

I didn't want to go to the school gates, so I asked a friend Nikki, who I knew I could trust to take Lucy to school and to collect her again for me. I would explain why when I saw her.

I didn't want anyone to see me and ask questions, or to put any pressure on Lucy.

Meanwhile, Luke could go to school with his mates as usual. I gave him a hug and told him everything would be fine, reminding him of how much I loved him.

We all agreed that we would keep quiet and that this was our secret. Nobody must know.

We arrived at Nikki's house wearing a hat and sunglasses, stilling feeling shaken and trembling.

I pasted a smile on my face and reassured Lucy that I would pick her up later from Nikki's house. She was quiet but nodded and showed me that she was ok with that.

Nikki's face, however, said it all. Her mouth dropped open in shock as she exclaimed what the hell has happened?

I said please don't ask, please don't or say anything, just look after Lucy for me today.

I had tears in my eyes and I could not speak.

I gave Lucy a hug and a kiss and told her I loved her and would see her later.

Nikki asked where I was going, and I told her I had a work meeting.

She said in horror you can't go looking like that look at the state of your face.

I thought I had done a good job of covering the bruises up, but obviously, I wasn't fooling anyone.

I drove for about an hour to get to my meeting, but how I got there I don't know. My mind was anywhere and everywhere else. I must have driven on autopilot.

I walked into the meeting and everyone went silent, you could have heard a penny drop.

I tried to be upbeat and break the silence.

Instantly, my manager Jill took me to one side and said I should be at home.

I said that's the last place I want to be.

Jill asked if I had gone to the police.

I said no, I was too scared. That he had threatened to kill me.

She persisted. You must go for the sake of your children.

One of my work colleagues tried to lighten up the mood with a joke asking if I had been in a fight with Mike Tyson.

I froze and felt sick, completely speechless, but I should have known they would be able to see through my disguise and know what had happened.

The meeting began, normality resumed.

I shouldn't have come, I realised only then how I must have looked.

During our lunch break, I had a phone call from Luke's school saying I needed to get to the school office as soon as possible.

Luke would be waiting there for me.

I asked why? What had he done?

They said nothing had happened at school, it was about what had happened and what had been done to me.

Luke had to stay in school as it wasn't safe for him or any of us to go home.

Luke had told them what had happened, and he was scared for me.

I explained to Jill what was going on and asked to leave early. I told her, I was worried about Luke.

Jill said of course and said she would give me a call later at home.

As I was driving to Luke's school, I was worried about what they are going to say filling my head with questions about what they had meant and why our home wasn't safe anymore.

As I arrived at Luke's school, I went to reception and said that I had come to collect Luke.

The receptionist notified the head teacher, Mrs. Brown, that I had arrived.

I was taken to her office where she and Luke were waiting.

Luke looked so worried and immediately launched into a stream of apology, crying I'm sorry Mum, but I had to say something, I'm so scared.

I said it wass ok, that, everything will be fine.

Mrs. Brown's faced was shocked as she stared at me, then sheshe told me to sit down and explained that we couldn't go home as it wasn't safe for us.

Now that what Luke had said had been confirmed by the state of my face, I could see she was trembling.

She said it was her duty of care to put the children first and that if I didn't notify the Police, she would. They would be taken into care.

Social services would be involved.

Our home was not a safe place to be.

I was shocked and stunned. We had done nothing wrong and that house was our home.

But I had no choice, I didn't want my children being taken away from me.

Mrs. Brown asked where Lucy was. I said she was at my friend Nikki's house.

All I had wanted to do was keep them safe and protect them.

Mrs. Brown called the Police and soon they were on their way to the school.

I phoned Nikki to tell her what was happening.

I said I would pick Lucy up after I had spoken to the police and that we would all have to go the station to make a statement.

The police arrived at the school and Luke told them again what had happened.

I couldn't talk about it, I felt sick and couldn't stop trembling with fear, as he relayed and talked his way through what he had seen that night.

The police said they would follow me to collect Lucy and then escort us to the police station to make a statement.

I was worried as Lewis always rang at 7pm to check that we were ok.

He would be suspicious if I didn't answer.

The police said that we could not go back home as it wasn't safe, if we did, it could happen again.

The police said that in these domestic violence cases, an abuser who has done it once, finds it much easier to repeat a second time.

The police officer said they would take us home and help us pack a bag for a couple of nights.

Meanwhile, they would find us a women's refuge to stay in.

I asked what a women's refuge was. The office told me it was a safe house, where we could stay and be safe until Lewis was arrested.

We can take your full statements in a couple of days once you're settled.

I was in shock, I didn't understand what was happening, but went along with it as I had no choice, if I wanted to be with my children.

I told Luke and Lucy what was happening and told them to pack a bag as if we were going away for a weekend with some games and toys.

The police escorted us back to the house in unmarked cars. so the neighbour's did not take any notice on what was going on.

I left my car parked up, then went into the house with the children to pack some bags, while the police waited for us.

I just chucked the essentials into an overnight bag, not really thinking about what I needed, as I did not know. I couldn't think.

I helped Lucy and tried to make light of the situations, saying we were going on an adventure for a couple of days.

We packed toiletries, nightwear, underwear, and a couple of casual outfits.

One of the policemen came in to check on us at one point and saw the punched door and stains of blood over the bedroom floor, cupboards, and bed.

He said they would be taking photographs of this as evidence.

I had not been able to sleep in that bedroom since that night.

I had shared Lucy's bed with her.

I could not face being in that bedroom; it was like something out of a horror movie to me.

I did not want to remember that night.

That night was the last time I saw my house as a home, for now it had become a crime scene of drugs and domestic violence.

The police took my house keys as I would not be needing them in the near future.

Luke, Lucy and I all got into the back seat of a police car and huddled together.

We drove away quietly and quickly into the darkness not knowing where we were going.

Leaving the house of horrors behind us.

CHAPTER 7

REFUGE NO1

The Police took my mobile phone and photographed all the texts that I had been sent in the time leading up to the incident.

I wanted to delete them, as every time I looked at my phone it would remind me.

But they were was evidence against Lewis, showing that everything he had done was all premeditated.

After that, I turned my phone off, as he always rang me at 7 pm.

I would not be speaking to him again.

As we got into the back of an unmarked police car, we cuddled up together, frightened.

We drove through the night into the unknown, not knowing where we were going or what was happening.

I was scared of the unknown but felt safer than I had in a long time, as we were with the police.

I reassured Luke and Lucy that we were safe now and could not return home, as it was not safe to be there anymore. As their Dad could come back and do it again, anytime.

What I didn't realise was that we would never return to that house again. It would never be our home anymore.

We arrived at a big country looking house, after about an hour in the car.

We drove up a long driveway, with tall trees flanking the drive on either side.

It didn't matter what time it was or where it was, all I knew was that we had arrived at a women's refuge and we would be safe.

I had a thousand questions… after all, I didn't know anything about this place.

What happened here? How long were we to stay here? Who else lives here?

We carried our bags through the door and into a long corridor, where we were told to wait.

We were then asked if we would like a drink or something to eat.

I refused the food, but the hot chocolate was welcomed.

Luke and Lucy wanted something to eat, I had forgotten that we hadn't eaten since lunch.

They were shown where the kitchen was, while I went into the office and the manager told me to take a seat.

I couldn't stop trembling; it was getting worse. I could barely hold the hot chocolate for fear of spilling it.

Mrs Sullivan, the manager, said I was most probably still in shock from the beating. That my reaction was completely normal and understandable.

I felt like a walking skeleton, totally dead inside. I was still in a state of traumatic shock.

She explained that we could stay here for as long as we needed, that this was a safe house for us, for as long as we wanted it.

We would get all the help and support we needed to get through this trauma.

The police would return and get full statements from Luke and me in a couple of days when we had settled in.

They wanted to take some photos of the bruising that covered my body and take some close up shots of my face, which was still multi coloured with bruises.

We were shown to our bedroom, which was the size of a double bedroom with bunk beds and a single bed, a sink and a portable TV fitted to the wall.

We had to share the toilet and bathroom, with the other residents on the same landing.

It was very quiet, and I didn't know how many other people were staying here.

We found it hard to sleep at first, even though we were all exhausted.

Luke slept on the top bunk, while Lucy and I slept together on the bottom bunk.

Lucy clung to me and cuddled into me, crying herself to sleep.

Luke wanted the TV on, so I let him, even though I couldn't normally sleep with the TV on.

But my mind was working overtime, and the TV was a welcome distraction.

I think I finally fell asleep through sheer exhaustion, as my body started to relax, knowing we were safe.

We woke up the next morning, with no idea what time it was, remembering where we were after a few seconds of confusion.

We were all shattered, not having had much sleep.

We unpacked our bags and found some toiletries and towels in the room.

Lucy and I went to find the showers and toilet, while Luke stayed in the room.

We waited our turn, then got showered and dressed.

I felt dirty and so unclean, I knew it was going to take me forever to feel and get clean again.

We went downstairs for breakfast, not knowing what to expect.

We were shown into the kitchen, being told that we all had our own cupboards with a lock and key.

We also had a shelf in the fridge and one shelf in the freezer.

The staff would do our shopping for us, as we could not go out.

I wanted to cry, my body felt weak, but I had to hold it together.

I had to keep remembering that we were safe and together.

The children were then shown the communal TV room, which had books and board games.

There was a garden with a swing and a slide.

This would be our home!!

But still, this house felt like a prison, as we could not leave the house or the garden.

Our freedom had been taken away from us.

Luke and Lucy could not go to school and I could not go to work.

The first week we were kept busy, giving statements, and being photographed.

I was being told about the procedures and what to expect.

I wanted to prosecute but at the same time was terrified of being in the same room as Lewis.

The police wanted Luke to stand up in court with me to make a statement.

I said he couldn't and wouldn't do that, Lewis was still his dad.

We finally agreed that we would do a video -link to give our statements, if Lewis continued to plead not guilty.

It seemed so unfair that Lewis was out there, living his life and enjoying his freedom, while we were still inside our new prison.

While Luke was becoming angry and aggressive, Lucy had become withdrawn and was not talking to anyone. All she did was draw and colouring.

Lucy expressed herself in her drawings and paintings.

Our shopping was done every week for the staff.

I told the staff that we needed to go out and have some space and be like a normal family.

The staff agreed to drive us all to a beach about 40 minutes away.

When we were in the car, it felt like we were in a movie watching the world go by, but we weren't part of it.

Luke and Lucy were excited to be outside and to be free. We were having a day out like a normal family.

It was the first time I had seen mythe children smiling and laughing in a long time.

They were running in and out of the sea, even though it was cold.

Luke and Lucy played in the sand and collected shells all day., Wwe even had an ice-cream.

We all walked along the beach and enjoyed breathing in the sea air, feeling free and alive once more.

The tears were streaming down my face, as I watched them chasing each other.

I wanted us to be that normal family again. I didn't want to go back.

Then it was time to return to the refuge, though we were allowed to get our shopping on the way home before we left the beach.

Luke and Lucy chose what they wanted to eat and picked up some treats.

We all got into the car and nobody spoke as we headed back to the refuge.

I had to do something, we couldn't go on living like this. It wasn't healthy and it wasn't normal.

I wanted our lives back.

As we returned to the safehouse, we felt exhausted but uplifted. The children asked if we could go again soon.

I thanked the staff and said we were very grateful, and that we appreciated what they were doing for us.

I spoke to the staff and said the children needed more freedom and needed to go back to school.

As I spoke to the staff, I broke down, sobbing, saying How could I let this happen? Why wasn't I stronger? I felt so guilty.

I never thought this would happen to me.

It felt like it was happening to another family, not us. Things like this didn't happen to me.

I was so angry that Lewis still hadn't been arrested, that the police were having trouble finding him.

He must have been in hiding.

The next morning, I received a telephone call from the police informing me that they had arrested him, but he was out on bail, as he said it was only a slap, he had given me!!

Unbelievable, I was furious. How could they let him go after our statements and photographs as proof?

Lewis had his freedom when he was guilty, and we were innocent.

The police said they were watching him and just waiting for him to slip up.

But it didn't make sense, and it felt like the justice system had let us down.

The police said that until he pleaded guilty, nothing could be done, but as he was on bail if he did anything wrong he would be arrested as soon as he did anything else wrong.

They said he had a colourful record and they were fully aware of his wrongdoings.

Lewis' solicitor had advised him that domestic violence victims never go through with court appearance, as they were usually too be terrified of seeing their abuser in court.

So, he believed he would not be convicted. But what he didn't know was that we could do it via video link.

I knew Lewis, I knew, he would be laughing at us and feeling pleased with himself, thinking he had won.

It suddenly hit me that, we were domestic violence victims, victims of a heroin addict, victims of the justice system.

I was gutted, devastated, how had this happened?

How can this get any worse?

As he was still out on bail, with no fixed address, the system was unsure of his whereabouts.

The only way we could have our freedom was to move to another refuge in a different county.

We had to move out of the area, but at least that meant the children could have their freedom and go to school.

We could do our own shopping and we could go out together as a family.

For us, it would be better than where we were now.

But it would mean leaving everything and everybody behind.

Including family and friends, we could not go back home or stay in the area.

Mrs Sullivan called me to her office to discuss the different options and areas we could go to.

We had a choice of cities to go to, and there were a couple of options with independent one-bedroom flats within a refuge so we could live independently, instead of sharing a double bedroom.

But it would cost more money.

Mrs Sullivan thought the one bedroom flat would suit us better as I wanted to go back to work if I could eventually. Apparently, I was not the typical domestic violence victim type, if there even was such a thing. We were not the norm.

I asked why I had to pay when I wasn't working, how could I pay?

Mrs Sullivan advised me that because I had a mortgage and worked, I was not entitled to any benefits.

But she did advise me to cancel my council tax payments and take a mortgage holiday payment for about 3 months, as my house was empty. It would be staying empty until I decided what to do.

I had to phone the utility companies and to say the house was empty. I also had to cancel my direct debits for the time being.

That way I would be able to afford the next refuge.

If I had been on benefits, I wouldn't have had to pay at all. It seemed unfair.

Paying for somewhere we didn't want to be.

Mrs Sullivan asked if I could drive and if I felt strong enough to drive.

I said yes, absolutely, but why?

She said once I had spoken to Lucy and Luke about the options, the police would escort us to the house in an unmarked car, so that we could collect our car and a few more belongings to take with us.

I would have to drive to the refuge, armed with a postcode and a telephone number to call.

Mrs Sullivan said to take as much as we could with us, to load the car up.

The police would help us and stay with us until we left the area.

I spoke to Lucy and Luke and they both said they would like it if we lived in our own flat and not have to share anything with anyone.

I explained it would still be in a refuge setting, but we would be more independent.

We would have our own kitchen/diner, bathroom, and a family bedroom.

Bunkbeds and a single bed. This was better.

Now we had decided where to go and when, all we had to was to pack.

The next morning Luke, Lucy and I were up early to pack up our overnight bag.

We waited anticipation, knowing we were going back to the house for the first time since the incident.

The police collected us from the refuge, waited while we said our goodbyes and watched as we thanked the refuge staff form all for their support.

Mrs Sullivan wished us all the best.

As we got into the police car, we looked back, knowing we would never return.

As we got nearer to our house, it felt strange seeing the house again.

The police gave me the keys and we went in through the back door.

The house smelt musty as no-one had been here for over 3 weeks.

I told Luke and Lucy to grab some suitcases and sports bags and to fill them up with their clothes, games, PlayStation, and toys and anything else they want.

We needed to take a TV, bedding, towels, and kitchenware, as I wasn't sure what would be there.

We loaded the car with as much as we could, everything and anything, that it was possible to take.

We were so busy packing that I didn't take any notice of the bedroom or the punched door.

I didn't know what would happen to the house, or if we would ever come back.

I felt sad that our final memories of this house were so unpleasant.

Luke and Lucy were done quickly, and ready to go...

We said our goodbyes and thanked the police for all their help and support.

They gave us the promised postcode and a telephone number.

The Police also said that they would keep an eye on the house, as it would be empty.

We drove away from the house silently, each of us lost in our own memories and thoughts.

Mentally saying goodbye to a chapter which had once been so full of life and love.

CHAPTER 8

REFUGE NO2

As we pulled onto the motorway, we stopped at a Mcdonalds, in a service area for a quick break.

It felt surreal that we could suddenly go where we wanted, walk around and buy whatever took our fancy.

The children were excited about this, it almost felt like we were on holiday.

After the stop, we drove for another couple of hours, during which time Luke and Lucy fell asleep.

It felt like I hadn't driven for months, like the old me was a lifetime away.

As we got closer to the postcode, I pulled over into a layby and phoned the telephone number for more directions.

Luke and Lucy woke up and asked if we were there yet.

I said nearly, we just have to follow these directions.

As we got closer, we saw the building was huge, with big iron gates leading up to the entrance.

The security camera was focused on us as we drove towards the gates, and spoke into the intercom and said who we were.

We drove into the car park and parked up.

We looked at each other. Buoying us all up, I said here we go, at least we will have our own flat with some privacy here.

We were met at the entrance by a member of staff and were shown straight to the office.

The entrance was narrow, and it opened up into a hallway with an office.

I filled in some paperwork and then Mrs Holloway, the manager, showed us to our flat.

It was on the first floor, next to the laundry room. Those were the only items we had to share with other residents.

There were two washing machines and tumble dryers on each landing.

The space we were to live in was smaller than I imagined but still plenty spacious, with a large bedroom complete with bunk beds and a single bed, with a wardrobe and a chest of draws.

A small galley kitchen/diner say off the main bedroom. The space was completed by a small lounge and bathroom.

There was a food hamper waiting for us with all the basics in.

Luckily, I had also seen a supermarket nearby, so we could do our own shopping.

Mrs Holloway gave us our keys, one for the flat and a keycode for the entrance.

She said she would let us unpack and settle in, and would come and see us tomorrow.

I could hear voices and noise coming from the flat next door as we walked down to the car and started to unpack.

This Refuge was full and busy with families.

As we unpacked, reality hit us that we were still not free.

Even with our own place, we felt like prisoners, with rules and regulations to abide too.

We unpacked as I tried to make our flat homely.

We decided to go shopping and get some nice food and treats in.

It was the first major shopping trip I had done in over 3 weeks.

It felt strange being a normal shopper in a supermarket, though at the same time it was nice to feel safe, knowing that we were miles away from home.

Luke set up the TV in the bedroom and one in the lounge.

I made the beds up and Lucy unpacked her toys and bags.

We all had showers in our bathroom which was a luxury, as we didn't have to rush and clean it every time we used it, before and after, like we had done at the other refuge.

Luke went on his PlayStation, Lucy was watching a film and I just chilled, feeling fragile and exhausted but relaxed.

Lucy and I had an early night, Luke came in later.

Luke had the bunk beds to himself, as Lucy still wanted to sleep with me.

We were all still having nightmares, and would wake up at different times of the night.

Lucy would cry in her sleep and shake, Luke would shout out, calling his dad's name to stop and start sweating.

I would wake up sweating, trembling, and reliving that night.

None of us had a good night's sleep, but that was the norm now, never mind being somewhere new and having to get used to another system.

We all slept in the next day and decided we would explore the area. I would also ask about the local schools.

Mrs Sullivan wanted to see us today as well, to give us more information about the refuge.

I had to do some shared cleaning on a rota basis for my landing and the laundry room every week.

We had to be in by 9 pm every evening. And no alcohol was allowed.

All the children went to the same primary and secondary school from the refuge.

The children would be registered by the refuge, and we could go for a school visit the next day.

I had an appointment at Luke's school and one for Lucy's school.

We all attended both schools, with my main priority being to support my children who were very nervous and scared about starting a new school.

I had a chat with both of their new headteachers and explained that we had just arrived and could the children start the following week.

71

I explained that they were very anxious, and that I needed to get their school uniforms.

It would give us all a chance to settle in, relax and catch up on some well-needed rest, as we were all exhausted with the transitions and events that had happened over the last few weeks.

They both agreed and Luke and Lucy were set to start the following Monday.

We manage to settle into the refuge and had some sort of normality pinned down within days.

If you could call it that, anyway. I didn't what was normal any more.

Over the next few days, we also explored the area and found some nice walks, discovered parks to play in and went shopping.

We felt free at last and began to do all the normal things that had been taken away from us.

We started to laugh and enjoy being outdoors, and for me it was good just watching the children be themselves again.

It was only when we went back to the refuge that I was it reminded of why we were here.

Luke, Lucy and I started to meet other families in the refuge, and they started to get involved with the other children, which helped as they were all going to the same schools.

I wasn't keen on getting too friendly with the other families, as all they talked about was what happened to them and it seemed like a competition, who had suffered the most and for the longest, who had been living in refuge housing for the longest.

Some families had been here two or three times and had raised their children in there.

I decided this wasn't going to happen to me, I wanted to be out of this place as soon as it was safe to do so.

For me, it wasn't a healthy setting for the children, it was depressing and full of negativity.

In the meantime, I was thinking about going back to work. I thought I could get a transfer if there was a vacancy.

I could not stay in the refuge all day while the children were at school, I knew I would go crazy.

I needed to be out and meet other people and to keep my mind occupied.

I phoned my manager Jill to tell her that we had to move out of the county to be able to have some freedom and independence while Lewis was on bail.

I told her we had moved to another refuge and that the children would be going to the local school.

I asked Jill if there was any chance of a transfer and if there was a position free within the company I worked for.

Jill had been very supportive and understanding, as had been the company I worked for.

I explained that I needed to go to work as I couldn't spend all day in the refuge while the children were in school, even if they could find me something else to do.

I asked Jill to keep our location confidential until Lewis was arrested.

We had been advised not to speak to our family or friends for the time being and not to speak about our past or where we used to live.

Nobody asked about personal details in the refuge, only how and why you came to be there.

The atmosphere in the refuge was tense and angry like everyone was about to explode.

Which, I suppose, was understandable considering none of us knew what the future held.

I was starting to fall even deeper into depression and was feeling suppressed and so were the children.

We were all sleep-deprived, as we were desperate to sleep, but scared to sleep because of the nightmares.

Also, the noises and arguing that we could hear from the flats next door would keep us up for hours on end.

Children were always running up and down the corridors screaming and crying, and TV's blared at all hours.

We tried to keep ourselves to ourselves, but everyone wanted to know your business, I think due to boredom more than anything else.

I didn't like to be too involved with the other families and kept out of their way, but it was difficult as Luke and Lucy made friends and they all went to school all together.

I was still very nervous and jumpy, though the bruises on my face were slowly going down and the swelling had gone.

Meanwhile, back home, Lewis was still in denial, still pleading not guilty, and maintaining that he had only slapped me.

Even though the police had photographic evidence.

He was playing for time, hoping that I would back down and not follow through with the court case.

Lewis knew I would not put the children through that, and would normally be right, but in this case, I had to show the children that what he did and had put us through, he could not be allowed to get away with it.

The staff in the refuge said that I wasn't the typical domestic violence case.

I was stronger, I was different, I was trying to focus on being positive and I wanted to go back to work.

The families in here were on benefits and I was the only one that had a mortgage and wanted to work.

It was so hard trying to stay positive surrounded by the negativity and stories of violence that filled the corridors all the time.

But I had to make out that everything was going to be fine and that we would leave here one day and have a family home again.

Even if I didn't believe it myself, but I had to tell myself it would be.

I didn't want to be a victim, I wanted my life back and to survive this ordeal.

We were all going to get through this. However long it took.

We were the three musketeers, that was what I told Luke and Lucy.

At last, I had some good news, I was able to get a transfer and start work.

It was the best news yet, I suddenly felt uplifted, like there was light at the end of the tunnel.

So, on Monday morning, we all got dressed, had breakfast and left altogether.

While Luke walked to school with the other children in his age group, I walked Lucy to school, then walked back, to get my car and drive to work.

I had to get directions to my new place of work, and while I was driving, I felt so many different emotions, from fear to excitement.

As I was driving, I felt like, for the first time in six weeks, we finally had some sort of routine and normality.

We were all away from the refuge for six hours.

Jill had arranged for me to workdo school hours Mon-Fri, so I could be there to pick Lucy up from school after work.

I was so lucky to have an amazing manager who supported me all the way through.

Luke and Lucy were anxious that I was going to work, in case Lewis would find me.

I explained to them that he wouldn't as we were in a different county now, and he did not know where we were. Also, I was in an office surrounded by people, so I would be safe.

It was like we had disappeared overnight in the eyes of everyone else that knew us.

That first day at work was the first time in about six weeks the children and I had been separated. We all felt nervous.

But at least life was going in the right direction, moving forward.

The children needed to go to school, and I needed and wanted to go to work.

Luke especially was feeling especially claustrophobic being in the refuge, in a small flat, and needed to get back to playing football and rugby, being able to release his anger and frustration.

Also, their brains needed some positive stimulation as I knew they both used to enjoy school.

After a couple of weeks, though, it all started to go wrong. Luke started to get bullied in school, because he lived in a REFUGE.!

And it wasn't just him so did the other children. I felt disgusted and angry, he had been through enough, he didn't need this.

Luke was very sensitive and caring, and had never experienced this before.

I couldn't believe how cruel children could be.

Luke's behaviour changed and he started to become aggressive, and refusing to go to school.

I went and spoke to his teachers and they said they would keep an eye on him and give him some counselling if he needed it.

The problem was where we lived, the circumstances and the noise.

I had to clean the corridors and laundry room at the weekends, and we had a time slot to be able to use the washing machine and tumble dryer. For any extra washing I wanted to do, I had to wait until everyone had done theirs and wait for a time slot.

So, I used to get up really early in the mornings or later in the evening to get mine done.

I wanted my own home again and the children to have their own bedrooms, to have our own space.

To be able to have their friends over and behave like normal children.

Especially for Luke as he was a teenager, and it was unhealthy for us to be living in the same room.

It was temporary, as the refuge advised us that we would be rehoused, but that thisit could take at least six months.

I couldn't wait that long. This situation wasn't doing our mental health any good.

It was different for me, as I already had a house and was not on benefits, so it was suggested I should sell my house.!

I was grateful for the refuge and I was grateful for being safe, but we needed our own routine and to get back to our way of life.

Everyone moans about routine, but when it is taken away from you without any choice, you suddenly feel like you haven't got any control over your life anymore.

Routine somehow makes you feel safe, secure, and normal... whatever those words mean. I didn't know anymore.

CHAPTER 9

NO GOING BACK

I had to make a decision about my house.

But what could I do?

How could I sell my house without advertising it?

I had been advised that I would never be able to go back home and live in that house, as I would always be at risk.

I had already realised that I had to make us a new home, and build a new life in a different county.

Miles away from my family and friends.

Thinking about it, would I want to go back to that house with all those memories? Not really.

But I would still like to go back to the area where we used to live. The area that was home.

At the moment, I had to accept that this was not possible while Lewis was still on bail.

In fact, it probably wouldn't be possible even for the immediate future.

But I had to learn to turn this negative into a positive and think of our immediate future.

First on the agenda was finding an estate agent that would privately put my house on the market and sell it discreetly for me.

I phoned my solicitor who had given me the advice so far, advised me and asked her if she could recommend an estate agent that would be discreet and understanding.

If Lewis knew I was selling it, he would harass the estate agent to find out where we were and would eventually know we had left the area.

Mr Jenkins phoned me and discussed the market value and I said I would post a set of keys to him so he could take some photos and do the viewings.

He was very supportive and understanding, telling me he would sell via word of mouth, among his contacts.

Confidentiality was a premium.

Mr Jenkins said it shouldn't be a problem, as the houses in that area were sought after anyway.

We agreed on a price and the nearest offer we would accept.

When the conversation was over and I hung up, I knew that was it, no going back.

I discussed with Luke and Lucy thewhat decision I had made, and the knowledge that we couldn't go back.

I said we might be able to return to the area in the future, but not at the moment while their dad was still on bail. We would also never be able to go back to our old house, as he would always be looking for us there.

The realisation and mixed emotions hit them at once, knowing that they would never see their dad again and would never go back to their childhood home again.

Luke was more upset than Lucy because of all his friends, but I said that once this was over, he could contact them again in the future and invite them over as much as he liked.

They understood but were grieving, as for them it was like losing their dad forever.

I was hoping by then, he would have made new ones and moved on.

But I did have an idea, some good news for them.

As I was working and my position was permanent, I thought we could look for somewhere to rent and make a house our new home again.

I suggested we could rent a house and move out of the refuge and start living again.

Luke was ecstatic, as he was still being bullied about where he lived.

You both can both have your own bedroom, and we can start a new life here.

Luke and Lucy were overjoyed and excited, and wanted to know when.

I told them we could start looking straight away.

I knew the maximum rent that I could afford and that we would like a 3-bed room house with a garden and parking.

I wanted a home and to be free, independent and back in control of my own life.

Not to live in fear and be surrounded by fear at every turn.

I spoke to a member of staff in the refuge and asked if she knew of any houses to rent.

I wanted somewhere quiet and safe.

She was shocked that I wanted to leave the refuge after only a month.

She said it was too early to leave, as we were all still distraught and need counselling.

I said that Luke and Lucy were going to have counselling at school, and explained that Luke was being bullied because he lived in the refuge.

I said he was becoming aggressive because of this and we needed to leave.

The manager finally agreed to support us as she could see my point of view.

She said I wasn't the typical victim of Domestic Violence and that I had guts, for leaving. I knew she was right and felt proud for the first time in a long time.

That afternoon after school, we all went to the estate agents and put our names down for 3 bedroom houses to rent.

I said we were available to move in as soon as possible.

I said we would rent and stay for as long as we needed to, to have some stability, to heal and to live as a family again.

I didn't want to uproot my children from school again, and hoped that Luke would settle down and the bullying would stop once he had his own family home.

We would give this town a chance and see how we go.

Luke and Lucy both started to make friends in the school outside the refuge.

Once we moved, they knew they would be able to have friends over to the house for sleepovers.

Luke was very sensitive but very angry, but I was hoping he would be able to get back into his sports and find ways to release his anger.

Lucy was very quiet, nervous and withdrawn, so I was desperate for her to have her own space of peace and tranquility again.

They were so different in their attitudes and actions. Luke was very vocal, while Lucy was so quiet and liked her own space.

Me, I was a walking skeleton, who was nervous and feared the unknown.

But I was also strong, determined, and independent. I was not going to let Lewis control me or our lives from a distance.

We were going to get through this. I wasn't sure how long it would take, but I knew we would get our lives back on track.

The first part of that was to find somewhere to live, and to make a home again.

To feel safe, to be able to relax, to have our own kitchen and bathroom and not have to share.

To be able to come and go as we pleased and not have a curfew.

To have a clean and tidy house, not having to clean up after anybody else.

To have our own bedrooms. Then, finally, the nightmares might start to dissipate, instead of haunting us in our sleep.

Being able to sleep alone with the lights off, instead of being afraid of the dark and being alone. That became the goal.

We started to view different properties, but couldn't find the right one.

They were either too expensive or only had 2 bedrooms.

I was paying nearly the same amount of rent to the refuge as I would be paying for a 2-bed house.

I kept being asked if I really knew what I was doing, being told it was still early days and we would not be as safe on our own.

I was willing to take the chance and my gut feeling was telling me it was the right thing to do.

We were in a different county and nobody knew where we were, so in my eyes we were safe.

For the first time in months, we were all excited and anyway, it couldn't get any worse.

Plus, there was an interest in my house, and my estate agent had found a buyer.

We just had to agree on the price and what was going to happen to the furniture.

I said to sell the furniture with the house, which the buyer was pleased about as they were first-time buyers, moving from a one bed flat.

My house was finally sold, but for a lot less than the going rate, mainly as I couldn't advertise it and wanted a quick sale.

I told Luke and Lucy that evening, that the house had been sold to a young couple.

Ultimately the timing couldn't have been more perfect, as that same evening I had a phone call about a 3 bed property that had come up for rent, and which would be perfect for us.

I made an appointment tofor viewing the following day after school.

It took the edge off from our house being sold, and gave us something to celebrate.

I collected both children from school and we all went straight to the address of the property.

As soon as I saw it, I knew it was perfect. It was in a cul-de-sac about 20 min walk from Luke's school.

The house had a parking space in a small drive, 2 double bedrooms, one with a double bed in it, and a single bedroom.

A small kitchen with a dining area and a lounge with patio doors opened into the south-facing garden.

The house had neutral decoration throughout and had just been decorated with new carpets, a gas fireplace and a large sofa in the lounge.

Fitted wardrobes graced all the bedrooms, alongside integrated kitchen appliances in the kitchen, meaning, I didn't have to buy much furniture.

We all loved it. It was as if the angels were finally looking down on us, and it was meant to be.

The rental was a new property on the market, so we could move in once all of the references were given and checked.

I was busy the next day getting a reference from my bank and my work, ready to send to the estate agent.

We were all so excited and started discussing what would go where and which bedroom each of us would have.

I went to the manager and paid my last rent payment for the refuge, it felt so good.

In a couple of weeks, we would be moving out of the refuge into our new home

We started to pack up and left the essentials only out to used up.

We were counting down the days.

Lewis was still pleading not guilty on the advice of his solicitor.

His solicitor advised him that the longer the case went, the weaker I would become and that eventually I would drop the charges.

The Police said that if I didn't stand up to him and follow through with the prosecution, he would be likely to do it again to someone else. Also, what message would it give to the children?

Especially the damage it would do to my son, telling him that domestic violence was not acceptable and not something to report.

I agreed to go to court with a screen or a video link, as I didn't want to be in the same room as him.

I was petrified of being in the same room as him or even in the same building, but still, I didn't want him to get away with it.

We had lost our home and our chosen way of life.

We were having nightmares, giving up family and friends and moving away from our home.

We had lost everything.

Now only that, but my children had lost their dad in the process.

Their feelings were in turmoil, stuck between a love and a hate filled relationship.

CHAPTER 10

NEW BEGINNINGS

The day finally came where we packed up our things and moved out of the refuge.

The refuge gave us a food parcel to get us started, plus a football for Luke and a painting set for Lucy.

They were very kind and wished us all the best, and their generosity felt quite overwhelming as we prepared to leave.

The refuge was a place where we knew we could go to be safe and protected, a place which gave you breathing space and support.

I knew I would always be grateful to them. Even so, this was a place I hoped I would never have to return to.

The manager of the refuge notified the police of our new address and landline number.

The police would come and check in on us once we were settled.

I knew the police were surprised that I was ever married to a man that could do something like this.

I was not what they expected.

I was not the typical drug dealer's wife.

Lewis had become an unsavoury character, and I was so much better out of his life completely.

As we unpacked and slowly settled in, getting used to our new lifestyle, we felt like we were on holiday.

We could go out whenever we wanted, we could have a long soak in the bath whenever we needed to relax, and the house was quiet, calm and relaxing all day and night.

We took long hot showers without having to clean it after every use.

I had my own washing machine and could do a wash whenever I wanted.

We had our own space inside and a lovely garden outside.

Luke and Lucy could finally have their friends over to stay, their home and they could go and visit friends when they wanted to.

We went around the local charity shops and recycling centres to buy them both bicycles, games, consoles and toys, and found Lucy a load of colouring stuff to keep her busy.

We also picked up some clothes and household goods along the way.

As time went on, we made the house our home and started to get back to our normal 9-5 routine.

We were all still having nightmares every so often, and Lucy would still sleep with me. At first, Luke would come into our room during the night too.

Lucy was still very quiet and withdrawn at school, though on the plus side Luke wasn't getting bullied as much and even started to cycle to school with his friends.

I was very nervous about this at first, as I was still having nightmares that his dad would kidnap him off the street.

You could say I was very protective over both of them, but it was more difficult with Luke as he wanted his freedom and demanded a right to stay out with his friends. This was of course understandable as he was growing up quickly and had seen more than an average teenager would ever see at his age. But still I worried.

He was still angry, and missed having a male role model in his life. He and his dad used to do a lot of activities together.

He also carried a lot of guilt and blamed himself for what happened, especially in telling the school about what happened.

He was torn between protecting me and being loyal to his Dad, by promising not to say anything.

Everyone told him he had done the right thing. His dad had to take responsibility for his actions and his choices.

Lewis had a lot to answer for.

They were both grieving in different ways, even though their dad was still very much alive.

They both knew it would not be safe to see him again and they would not be able too anyway, even if they wanted to.

Luke and Lucy thought they had lost their dad when we moved away but in reality, they had lost him a long time ago to drugs.

Heroin was his number one priority, that was his life, and ultimately it had led to devastating decisions and actions that affected our lives too.

With the house sold completely with all its furniture, eventually I could pay off the mortgage.

That sparked the end of a great and traumatic chapter in our lives.

It was coming up for six months since we had moved into our house, when I got the news.

Luke and Lucy had started to join in afterschool activities and immerse themselves more in school life, which was starting to build their self-esteem and confidence.

The news which finally arrived shared a court date and the news that the court case was still going to go ahead.

I confirmed I was still happy to testify and would said I would still go ahead and take the day off work and bring Luke out of school.

I hoped I had made the right decision for all of us.

As the date drew nearer, I received an unexpected call from the Police, saying that Lewis had pleaded guilty. His solicitor had advised him that it would not look good bringing his son, a minor, into court, and that this would make his sentence would longer and lose him favour with the jury.

The court case was dropped for us and Lewis was charged with extreme GBH.

Lewis was sentenced to 4 years in prison.

I thought I was going to faint both from shock and disbelief, but also relief.

I started to cry and then found myself sobbing uncontrollably.

I felt like an enormous weight had been lifted from my shoulders.

I suddenly felt extremely exhausted.

I couldn't thank the police enough, and for their continued support.

I suddenly felt truly free and liberated and felt some justice had been done.

Now I had to tell the children.

Luke was relieved that he didn't have to speak against hid dad, but angry and upset that he was in prison. He felt like he had put him there.

I told him that I did; that I was the one who filed the court case and pursued it.

Lucy was just quiet. All she knew was that she was safe with her Dad was locked up behind bars.

That night was the best night sleep I had, had in months.

For me, life became better and easier, but the children were still struggling, especially when it came to Father's Day.

In school, they were making cards and talking about their dads, and what a special day it was.

That was the first time that Lucy came home crying and saying she missed her Dad.

In fact, it was the first time she had spoken about her Dad.

I told her she could still make a card and that we would do something nice for the day.

We decided to go out for the day and forget about the sentiment of the day altogether. We went to the beach for a picnic and went swimming. We had fun in the amusements and treated ourselves to ice-cream. Then we topped the day off with fish and chips on the beach.

Even though we were surrounded by families with Dad's all around us, we still had a good time.

Something we hadn't done in a while.

Lucy fell asleep on the way home and Luke was very quiet, emotionally and physically shattered.

I thought that now would be a good time for both children to have some counselling, as we were settled and finally back in a family home.

I phoned both of their schools and spoke to the Principles at each, asking school for this to be organised.

The school suggested that all of us to have counselling as a family, but I wasn't ready to discuss what had happened to me just yet.

I just wanted to feel normal again and get back to being me.

It was too soon for me to talk about it.

I wanted the focus to be on the children, especially with how upset they were over Father's Day.

I wanted them to have their counselling during school hours, so it didn't seem like such a big deal to them or to their other friends.

Lucy had counselling through play and drew pictures of she felt.

Luke hated the counselling, hated talking to strangers, and still felt protective over his dad.

But I explained to him this was just a way of releasing his anger and discussing how he felt about what happened.

Luke kept saying that if he hadn't told his teachers, we would not be in this situation.

His dad would not be in prison.

I said he had saved my life by doing what he did, as his dad would have done it again.

I might not have survived the next time.

Luke wanted life to go back to normal, but it would never be the normal he knew again.

Luke was so much more affected than Lucy, purely because as he had seen and heard so much more.

Luke had seen things he shouldn't have seen and knew that a lot of what he had experienced was not normal for a 13-year-old.

Luke's counselling lasted for 3 months, with once session every fortnight, but it did not benefit him. So, we stopped it.

It was too soon, so I decided to leave the choice to him. He will decide when the time is right to talk about it.

Lucy took the counselling well and started to improve slowly and be herself again.

It took us all about 12 months after that night, to really start to relax and live again.

Time is a good healer and with time we did.

We will never forget, but we forgave.

We survived and became stronger individuals, with a stronger family bond.

Luke and Lucy are adults now, both with their own children.

It seems like another lifetime, a past life, one I choose to forget.

The children and I survived Domestic Violence and found a way to live a life.

There is always hope, trust, and belief in yourself.

Lewis did me a favour, he made me stronger and more independent.

For you are stronger than you think.

You are braver than you believe.

You are smarter than you think.

You are a survivor.

Printed in Great Britain
by Amazon